If You Leave,

# I Will Kill You!

Getting Off the *Beaten* Path of
Domestic Violence

If You Leave,

# I Will Kill You!

## Getting Off the *Beaten* Path of Domestic Violence

Erika Gilchrist

Other books available in the
Unstoppable Publishing's Library:

### The Secrets to Being an Unstoppable Woman
*Roll up your sleeves, make no excuses, and get what you want!*

### 10 Ways to Prevent Failure (Audio Book)
*A straightforward guide to help you stay focused on attaining your goals.*

### Starting Today
*365 Quotations to stimulate, inspire, and enhance your personal growth.*

### The Unstoppable Woman's Guide to Emotional Well-Being
*A book for women written by 23 female authors, coaches and professionals.*

### How to Write & Publish Your Book NOW!!
*Step by step guide to put you on the fast track to becoming a published author.*

### Success Guide for the Unstoppable Entrepreneur
*Straightforward guide to help new business owners and entrepreneurs excel in their business.*

# www.TheUnstoppableWoman.net

**Cover Design:** Sandra Ballenger
www.SandraBallenger.com

**Illustrator**: Arthur T. Pressley

# Acknowledgements

I could list names for days when it comes to this book – I thank those who I have interviewed who shared their traumatic stories of abuse so candidly. Without your perspectives, I would not have been able to offer so many options to the readers of this book who are seeking help.

I would also like to thank my good friend and colleague, Dr. Monika Black, for her insightful wit, passion for justice, and unwavering faith in the human spirit. It has inspired me beyond words to bring all that I have to this book so that it empowers the lives of generations long after I'm gone.

# Table of Contents

# **Introduction**

As a child who witnessed domestic violence, then experiencing it as a young woman, I have two unique perspectives on this epidemic. But it isn't enough to simply offer my perspectives when there are literally millions of people who are suffering from it as well. I wanted to present the facts and evidence-based practices as thoroughly as I could without losing the heart of the book - I also wanted to dig as deeply as I could into the very core of the human experience without eliminating factual premises. This guide has an ideal balance of them both.

As the title speaks to "Domestic Violence," you will notice that I refer to it as IPV within the text. This is because IPV is more versatile and is being widely used more frequently.

I have changed the names of those who have chosen to share their stories to protect their identity. But understand that they were fully aware that I was researching solutions for this book and they wanted to be part of that journey..._your journey_. They spoke with such love and compassion for you even though they may never meet you in person. I drew much strength from them and silently wished that I had that circle when I was on the path to escape.

You will find a list of helpful resources for yourself, or someone you love who needs it. It is my sincerest hope that this book reaches victims in time to make them vicTORS.

# What the Heck is IPV?

1

**IPV** is one of those acronyms that doesn't immediately spark ideas on what it can possibly mean. If you were asked your thoughts on it, you may start making educated [and some not-so-educated] guesses. But for those who are very familiar with the term, it can bring thoughts of sadness, anger, and even feelings of anxiety when they see it.

IPV – Intimate Partner Violence. This identifying term has evolved throughout the years. Some refer to the act(s) as *Domestic Violence* or *Domestic Abuse.* Because of the many changing faces of abuse, this term has been widely used to more accurately describe the horrific epidemic.

> *Intimate partner violence (IPV) is a serious, preventable public health problem that affects millions of Americans. The term "intimate partner violence" describes physical, sexual, or psychological harm by a current or former partner or spouse.*
>
> Centers for Disease Control & Prevention (CDC), 2015

Despite the interchangeable names, one thing certainly has not changed – these preventable and vicious acts have affected the lives of millions of men, women and children and it must be stopped through prevention, education, trauma informed care, and recovery efforts. One victim is too many.

## Why Would Anyone Want to Abuse Another?

When we think of assaults in a relationship that is supposed to be one of love and support, it's hard to fathom the reasoning behind bringing harm to someone who is significant to your life. But it happens – and it happens quite often. This brings us to the question at hand. Why on Earth would anyone want to abuse another? We can sum it up in a single word: **CONTROL.** Abusers want to maintain control of the inner workings of the relationship and this can only be accomplished by controlling the partner.

There are many contributing factors as to why abusers may think that it's okay to control their partner:

- o Perhaps they believe that an unequal relationship is ideal for them.
- o They feel helpless in other areas of their life (work, school, family, church...etc) and feel the need to control something.
- o A patriarchal societal influence has granted them the right to abuse.
- o They believe that they know what's best for the other person.

In any case, to deliberately oppress and dominate another human being for your own gratification is wrong and abusive.

**Forget What You Thought You Knew**
Before I educated myself about IPV, I thought I was well informed because of my personal experience with it. I figured that it was isolated in certain "types" of homes, communities, and economical brackets. As someone who grew up with limited financial resources, I could only speculate IPV from that particular lens, which prohibited me from seeing its influence on a much grander scale. As we go through the following myths, ask yourself if any of these are similar to what you may have

perceived.

**Myth 1 – IPV is very bad, but it's rare.**
An estimated 3 to 4 million women are physically assaulted each year in the United States.[1] This number doesn't even include the other forms of IPV which will be explained in detail later in this book. Also note that this estimated figure is based on the number of cases that have been reported. So it's safe to say that the actual number of women who are beaten and/or otherwise abused is much greater.

**Myth 2 – IPV is usually an isolated occurrence.**
Abuse of any kind tends to follow a pattern over time. The intensity can also increase over time if the abuser thinks that he/she is losing control of the other person's actions, thoughts, and feelings. By the time an incident is reported, the victim has likely been assaulted multiple times and now feels the need to seek help outside of the relationship.

**Myth 3 – Victims of abuse can just leave.**
This is one of the most common myths and hence, a major contributing factor in why many people who have not experienced IPV lack sensitivity to the situation. There are multiple reasons why the victim has chosen not to leave which is outlined in the chapter "Why Do People Stay?" But to offer more simplified reasoning – many victims have in fact tried to leave only to get more severely punished for doing so. Of the total domestic violence homicides, approximately 75% of the victims were killed as they attempted to leave the relationship or after the relationship had ended.[2]

**Myth 4 – It's up to the entire family to stop the abuse.**
Abusing another is a behavioral choice that can only be stopped

by the abuser. An abuser may be coerced by the victim's family to cease the behavior, but ultimately the decision to stop is made by him/her. In many cases, the family has been strategically isolated from the victim because of this reason. If abusers know that their partner has a strong support system, it would be more difficult to control them, so the ideal situation is get the victim as far away from their family as possible.

## Myth 5 – IPV only occurs in low income and poorly educated communities.

This myth is one that I admit to thinking. The community that I grew up in was not affluent, and it simply never occurred to me that this type of behavior happened in families who were. Nonetheless, IPV occurs across geographical, economical, educational, religious, and racial lines. It knows no boundaries. There are many reported cases of ministers, professors, doctors, community leaders, politicians, and other prestigious figures in society who are serial abusers.

## Myth 6 – Drug & Alcohol abuse causes IPV.

While drugs and alcohol may cause a higher likelihood of an assault, they are not the cause. The cause is still the abuser, period. There are many people who abuse drugs and alcohol who do not engage in IPV behavior. In fact, drug and alcohol use has been used as a crutch by abusers to coerce their partners into staying. They may give the impression that if the drinking stops, so will the abuse. This is NOT true. These are separate issues that should be addressed accordingly.

## Myth 7 – Even if a man abuses, he is still a good father and should have partial custody of his children if the relationship fails.

70% of men who abuse their partners also sexually and/or

physically abuse their children. Children who witness abuse develop psychological damage as if they were actually abused directly. Also, the abuser may use the children as a means to remain closer to the victim in an attempt to control from a distance. While in the abuser's custody, children are often interrogated about the whereabouts and goings-on of the victim, which places added psychological stress on them.

## Myth 8 – Women are just as violent as men.

While violent tendencies cross gender lines, the vast majority of reported cases of IPV (around 95%) are women as victims. There's IPV in homosexual relationships as well.

## Myth 9 – IPV is not a serious issue in the U.S.

Battering is the single largest cause of injury to women in the Unites States. About **4,000** women die each year due to domestic violence - that's approximately 11 deaths each day. With numbers this staggering, it completely blows away this myth.

## Myth 10 – Abusers get violent simply because they're under pressure and lose their temper.

Abusers want to control the other person, PERIOD. If this myth were true, then the abuser would "lose their temper" and assault people at work, in social circles, and at religious affairs – all of which can be cesspools of pressure. The abuse only takes place with the partner, which indicates that the abuser is very well aware of when and where they can display this behavior unnoticed.

## Myth 11 – The abuser doesn't know how to show love and affection.

Contrary to this belief, it's the display of love and affection that lured the victim into the relationship. Abusers will not go out on a first date with someone and display abusive tendencies. The warmth and tenderness is intense in the beginning to entice the victim into a false sense of security.

**Myth 12 – When children witness abuse, they grow up to be abusers.**
Many children who witness IPV during their formative years experience multiple psychological and emotional struggles as they enter adulthood. Many of them use those occurrences as a reminder of what NOT to do in their own relationships.

Whether or not you are guilty of believing these myths or not is now irrelevant. You're aware of what's true and what is false when it comes to IPV. With these myths in mind, you can now shift your perception of what it means to be an abuser, a victim, or advocate.

If You Leave, I Will Kill You!

# The Sneaky Side of Abuse

2

Thus far, we have been referring to occurrences of IPV in its physical form of battering, which is the most recognizable by the human eye, and also the most frequently reported. This is partially due to the fact that the other forms of IPV can be so subtle, that many don't even realize that they're being abused. In fact, many women that I have coached throughout my career readily answer "No" to the question of whether or not they have been victims of IPV. But after hearing their stories of personal relationship woes, I quickly became conscious of the fact that they were indeed in an abusive relationship. Without revealing my findings, I would start to openly discuss my past personal relationship failures & lessons to offer a peek into what abuse really looks like in a non-physical realm. As a result, many of them self diagnosed their partnership(s) and were alarmed to realize that they too were former [or current] victims of IPV.

Having stated that, let's have a look at the many faces of IPV to draw a clearer picture of what it looks like. We'll start with the most commonly recognized form:

**Physical Abuse**

> *Physical abuse is any intentional and unwanted contact with you or something close to your body. Sometimes abusive behavior does not cause pain or even leave a bruise, but it's still unhealthy.*
>
> "What is Physical Abuse," © 2012 LoveIsRespect.org

This behavior can include, but is not limited to:
- o Scratching
- o Pushing

- o Hair pulling
- o Shoving
- o Throwing
- o Grabbing
- o Biting
- o Choking
- o Shaking
- o Slapping
- o Punching
- o Burning
- o Use of a weapon
- o Use of restraints, or one's body, size, or strength against another person

Basically, any object that can cause physical harm to another can be used to commit physical assault on a partner. This stage of abuse is usually on the back end of the abuse cycle. More subtle forms of abuse precede the bodily injury.

Battered women average 6.9 physical assaults by the same partner in a year. If we had to evenly average this statistic, the abuse would take place approximately once every 60 days.

Sarah* candidly explained to me that she was a model who would get hired quite frequently for regional fashion shows and other social events. This afforded her the luxury of not having to work a full time job. Her fiancé was well aware of how she earned her money, so he was very careful to never hit her in the face, as that would mean less money coming into the household [and less money for him to control]. She said he resorted to pinching, shoving, and hair pulling as a means of getting his message across.

"I was always afraid of bruises and bald scalp patches," she stated. "Once or twice I'd end up with a small scar that could easily be covered with body makeup, but in the back of my mind I prayed that he would not permanently scar me."

## Sexual Abuse

*Sexual abuse refers to any action that pressures or coerces someone to do something sexually they don't want to do. It can also refer to behavior that impacts a person's ability to control their sexual activity or the circumstances in which sexual activity occurs, including oral sex, rape, or restricting access to birth control and condoms.*

"What is Sexual Abuse," © 2012 LoveIsRespect.org

Some sexual abuse behaviors can include, but are not limited to:
- *Unwanted kissing or touching*
- *Unwanted rough or violent sexual activity*
- *Rape or attempted rape*
- *Refusing to use condoms*
- *Restricting someone's access to birth control*
- *Keeping someone from protecting themselves from sexually transmitted infections (STIs)*
- *Sexual contact with someone who is very drunk, drugged, unconscious, or otherwise unable to give a clear and informed "yes" or "no."*

When we think of a couple in a committed relationship, we often assume that if they are having sexual intercourse, that it's mutually consensual. I mean, anything else would be barbaric, right? It happens more often than we may think.

Most rapes committed against women are committed by an intimate partner (spouse, boyfriend/girlfriend) or someone else they know (friend, family member, acquaintance).

One woman, Tara*, who I interviewed about her IPV situation, stated that her ex-husband would hold her down to force her to have sex for hours at a time as a way of numbing his need for an alcoholic drink. He explained that it was either he drank, or he had sex, and often made the decision himself regardless of what she wanted.

"I felt so helpless," Tara stated. "The feeling of reluctantly giving yourself in that manner to a man who you despise is unimaginable. You feel angry, violated, and mortified all at the same time. But if I didn't want to be punished, I had to comply."

**Emotional/Psychological Abuse**

> *Emotional abuse is threatening a partner or his or her possessions or loved ones, or harming a partner's sense of self worth.*
>
> Center for Disease Control and Prevention, 2011

Examples include, but are not limited to:
- o Stalking
- o Name-calling
- o Intimidation
- o Isolating a partner from their friends or family
- o Public humiliation
- o Malicious withdrawal of affection
- o Saying mean things to you

- o   Doesn't allow you to make decisions
- o   Threatens you
- o   Ignores your feelings
- o   Puts you down
- o   Keeps you from sleeping
- o   Does things that make you feel crazy
- o   Tells you and others that you're crazy
- o   Tells you that your decisions are bad

Emotional and psychological scarring takes much more time to heal than physical scars do. Because this type of abuse does not appear in physical form, it can get overlooked; and sometimes, when it goes untreated, can cause psychological destruction and may rupture the chances of ever having a healthy relationship with anyone. It can show up as PTSD (Post Traumatic Stress Disorder), aggression towards another, extreme depression, and other psychological issues. What's worse is that many victims will carry on this behavior and not even realize the source.

> 48.4% of all women have experienced at least one psychologically aggressive behavior by an intimate partner.
>
> Breiding, M.J., Chen, J., & Black, M.C. (2014)

One may also use sarcasm, masked humor, or insincere compliments to belittle a partner like:

*"You're pretty cute to be so fat."*
*"I don't think you're ugly even though everyone else does."*
*"Go ahead and eat MORE food – that'll really turn me on."*

Ana* was a child who witnessed her disabled mother being belittled by her father regularly. At the age of 19, she left home in search of life less unstable and more balanced so she could thrive. But she noticed some behavior patterns in herself that hindered her ability to truly connect emotionally with others. She would get angry and verbally provoke her suitors to see if they would show any signs of extreme oral retaliation. "I didn't even realize that I was doing it," Ana admitted. "One day, a guy that I was dating told me that I had anger issues that were 'misdirected' and that I needed to figure out why." It was at that moment when she suddenly realized her pattern. "Because I was so hell bent on never becoming a victim like my mom, I created a monster who would test the waters first before the real me could be vulnerable. But in doing so, I'm sure I pushed away some men who may have been very good for me."

Ana, now in her late 60's, is married to a man who she describes as "patient beyond measure who could see right through me."

Another woman named Yolanda* found herself in a relationship where her abuser called her a "worthless bitch" so often, that it became her 'household name.' If she inquired about why she couldn't have a specific thing, or go to a particular place, he would glare at her and ask, "Why do you think?" To which she had to respond, "Because I'm a worthless bitch." If she didn't respond in that way, she would be punished.

Emotional abuse is catastrophic and its effects can last a lifetime.

## Verbal Abuse

*Verbal abuse refers to the use of language as a means to control or subordinate another person for either self-gratification or to impose one's view or will on another to gain an unfair advantage in resolving a dispute.*

*www.YourSocialWorker.com © 2010 Gary Direnfeld, MSW, RSW*

Some acts of verbal abuse may include, but are not limited to:
- o Hostile tone, volume, or intensity of delivery
- o Shouting
- o Yelling
- o Screaming
- o Or alternatively, talking quietly yet intensely so as to instill fear

Verbal abuse can be emotionally abusive as well. For example, the abuser may use the following statements in an abusive tone to instill fear:

*(Slow and deliberate tone)* **"You <u>will</u> be home by 8pm or else."**
*(Yelling)* **"How could you be so stupid?!"**
*(Screaming)* **"Don't you ever speak while I'm talking!"**

Cara* recalls her 4 year relationship with Bill* as one that made her to feel as if she walked on eggshells every day. He was a university professor who was accustomed to being the expert in the room, and whenever she had an opinion that differed from his, he would verbally bash her ideas. After a while, the verbal bashing turned from her ideas to her character, then to her daily actions.

"I was so afraid of making a mistake. I questioned everything from the color of my outfit to the choice of meal for the evening." She vividly remembers one night while preparing dinner; he stormed in shouting about why she parked her car in the garage when she knew that he would be home soon and wanted that space for his own vehicle. At that moment, she was handling a hot casserole dish that she has just extracted from the oven, and was so startled by his outburst, that she dropped the platter, splashing the hot cheese all over herself and the floor. This resulted in first-degree burns on her chest and legs. "I was a wreck inside. To this day, the sound of his voice makes my blood run cold. I'm so grateful to have gotten out of that relationship."

Constance* has a similar story. Her ex-husband Mike* was a newly ordained minister who, according to her, "Had a scripture for everything." He would use the Holy Bible as a way to control her actions. Constance stated, "I'm a religious woman as well, so the fact that he was so heavily involved in our church was very appealing to me. I enjoyed being counseled by him until we became seriously involved." She began to notice that his manner of delivery became more and more aggressive, almost to the point of shouting at the top of his voice. She stopped enjoying the [once] casual conversations about how to apply scripture to their lives because it shifted to a one-sided "this is how it's supposed to be and that's the end of it" type of discussion.

"Once I was awakened by the sound of him shouting the words 'No, no, no!' and I thought that someone had died. When he reached our bedroom he continued yelling, but it was directed at me about how I have sinned because the house wasn't 'in order.' It was around 2am, and I found myself cleaning my guest bathroom while being verbally bashed through biblical references of how a woman's position dictates a clean household at all times. I never slept soundly since that night."

Can you imagine being jolted from your slumber by someone you love who is screaming at you for something they believe you should have done? That's a very traumatic event that no one should experience.

## Economic Abuse

> *To limit a partner's access to assets or conceal information and accessibility to the family finances, which diminishes the capacity for the partner to support him/herself rendering them dependent on the abuser.*
>
> Adams, Adrienne; Sullivan, Bybee, Greeson (May 2008)

This may include, but is not limited to:

- o Giving an allowance & monitoring what's bought
- o Denying access to his/her own paycheck
- o Prevention of seeing shared bank accounts or records
- o Using the partner's SS# to obtain credit without the partner's permission
- o Refusing to give money, food, clothing, rent, or medication
- o Forbidding a partner to go to work or limiting their hours
- o Creating a situation that would cause a partner to become 100% dependent on them

This form of abuse can be very subtle, especially if one of the partners has proven to be a poor manager of finances. There's a thin line between monitoring the funds to avoid over spending, and rendering a partner completely dependent on the other.

> Between 94-99% of domestic violence survivors have also experienced economic abuse.
>
> Postmus, J., Plummer S., Mcmahon, S., Murshid, N., & Kim, M. (2011).

Alex* was a business owner who inherited the family's failing business. Unfortunately, Alex was not the most financially responsible person, and she relied on her accounting department to handle that aspect – until she married Jordan*. Jordan, although she had her own substantial amount of money, felt the need to scrutinize every penny that came into & out of their household.

"At first I was relieved that she was so good with money," said Alex. "That's one less thing I had to be concerned about. But then I noticed that if I wanted something simple – like a new hat or a sweater – she would get very agitated."

Jordan began implementing an allowance for Alex to manage, which made her uncomfortable. But for the sake of keeping the peace, she complied. But then the things that Alex purchased with her allowance were being analyzed. "She would ask me things like, 'Where's the receipt for the purchase you made yesterday?' or 'Let me keep your ATM card for the day.' Then I wouldn't ever see it again. It started to freak me out."

Jordan then escalated the control by withdrawing the allowance altogether and telling Alex that if she needed anything, she had to get that item approved. Jordan was especially guarded when it came to Alex's family asking for money. "I didn't come from money, so when my relatives would ask for a loan, it was usually less than a hundred dollars, which I knew we could afford, but Jordan wouldn't have it."

When Alex began to speak up about how the treatment made her feel, it seemed to make the situation worse, especially after Alex's business went under. She found herself asking for money for every single item that she wanted to buy – sanitary items, gas, food, grooming products…etc. "It was humiliating to ask my wife for $15 for tampons and pads. I had to get out of that situation." And she did just that.

The fact that Alex wasn't the best overseer of her money is no excuse to be financially abused. Regardless of how you are with the handling of your money, it's NEVER okay to have the access to it completely denied. Although Alex didn't mention any physical abuse, it's important to know that economic abuse often occurs simultaneously with physical or other forms of violence. It's an overlooked and extremely impactful form of abuse that happens to people every day.

## Digital Abuse

> *Digital abuse is the use of technologies such as texting and social networking to bully, harass, stalk, or intimidate a partner.*
>
> "What is Digital Abuse?" 2012 www.LoveIsRespect.org

Some tactics include, but are not limited to:

- o Dictating who can and cannot be Facebook friends
- o Sends negative, insulting or threatening emails
- o Using social media sites to keep tabs on partner
- o Pressure to send explicit videos or pictures

- o Steals or insists to be given passwords
- o Constantly texts to the point of fear of being away from the phone
- o Looks through phone frequently

Nearly half of all young people aged 14-24 report being electronically harassed in some form; 40% report incidences of digital dating abuse, and 11% have shared naked pictures of themselves.

Alyssa* made friends with someone on Facebook during her first year at college and soon thereafter, they met in person. Kyle* seemed very nice at first, but after a few dates, Alyssa quickly realized that he wasn't the one for her. In the weeks to follow, Kyle started sending her messages on Facebook pleading to see her again. When she refused, his messages turned dark. He started commenting about her posted whereabouts and how he will show up unexpectedly next time and she'd 'be sorry.' She reported him to Facebook, and then blocked him from her friends list. He then turned to emails with similar dark tones, and so she blocked him there as well. Then he started texting her with images of women being hanged and other gory acts.

Alyssa had enough and notified the local authorities because she feared for her life at that point. "He seemed so nice at first. I didn't know he'd be that crazy," Alyssa said. "I'll do a better job of screening boys before I go out with them, that's for sure." Alyssa was relieved to discover that the following year, Kyle was no longer attending the same college.

This scenario could have ended much worse. And unfortunately, many cases have a deadly end. We don't usually think of social media as an outlet for IPV, but it's the most accessible avenue to reaching multiple people in a very short period of time. It's an abuser's dream. Digital abuse can escalate very quickly and even be fatal when it's not handled immediately.

## Revenge Porn

> *Revenge porn is the posting, sharing, or publishing of **nude and/or sexually explicit** pictures/videos of a person on the internet without their consent, often accompanied by personal or identifying information.*
>
> http://nomore.org/dating-abuse-goes-digital-revenge-porn/

This is not **NEW**. In the 1980's, women sued Hustler Magazine for publishing their photos in the Beaver Hunt section without their permission. Several courts determined that publishing intimate photos without verifying whether the pictured women actually gave the go-ahead gave the false impression that all of the featured women felt comfortable with their pictures appearing in a "coarse and sex-centered magazine."

Revenge porn is digital sexual assault, and it is illegal in many states [*http://www.endrevengeporn.org/revenge-porn-laws*]. Although it may not involve physical assault, it violates a person's privacy, exposes them sexually, and brings immeasurable harm to the victim. Even though the photographs or videos may have originally been privately shared or taken with the victim's consent, the use of them later to embarrass them and violate that person's privacy, safety or dignity is incredibly damaging.

These forms of abuse happen to millions of men and women every day – the extent at which it can happen has varying degrees of severity, but all are considered abuse.

 If you're not fully aware of the many faces of abuse, it can creep its way into your relationship, bringing with it heartache, confusion, and feelings of inadequacy. There may have been a few types of abuse listed here that triggered thoughts of a previous [or current] relationship. Quite often when I speak on this topic, multiple people have deduced that they were in fact part of an abusive union. But now that you are aware, abuse can no longer sneak up on you unrecognized.

# If You Leave, I Will Kill You!

# How Did I Get Here?

3

"How did I get here?" is the question that I asked myself as I stared out of the window from the top bunk of a bed in a women's shelter from a bedroom that I shared with 5 other people. I reflected on all of my decisions that led to that moment. Some of them I wished I could change, and others I'd repeat. But despite my current situation, I found comfort in one thing – the _knowing_ that I would never be in that situation again. As I pondered my question, I had a few revelations...

## The "Weight Gain" Approach

(It sneaks up on you a pound or two at a time until you realize one day that you no longer fit the clothes you were once comfortable in)

I can recall an occasion approximately a year after my last abusive relationship ended. A woman called my office line and introduced herself as the new girlfriend of my ex-abuser. We'll call her "Jillian." I was very intrigued when I discovered who she was and had a strong desire to know the nature of her call. According to my recollection, the conversation went something like this:

**Jillian:** _Hi Erika, I'm the girlfriend of Winston* and I would like to talk to you if you have a moment please._
**Me:** _Yes, of course. How can I help you?_
**Jillian:** _First, I want to tell you that I found you online and I have reviewed your website. I think you're a beautiful person and I love what you're doing._
**Me:** _Thank you, I appreciate that._
**Jillian:** _Forgive me if this is intrusive, but I wanted to know how the relationship between you and Winston ended._
**Me:** _Poorly, why?_

*Jillian: Well, long story short, I had to call the police on him while my friends restrained him on my living room floor. When the police arrived, they discovered that he had a restraining order from his ex…you. That's how I got your name.*

She went on to explain details of the relationship they had up until that point, outlining all of the altercations, signs, and indicators that he was not a good fit for her. While she talked, I felt like I was in a time warp. I recognized and experienced those very same behavioral patterns and I found myself nodding and verbally agreeing with her frequently as she spoke. Then she asked a question that literally made me stand to my feet to answer. I found myself pacing as I responded.

*Jillian: Erika, how did a guy like that get two beautiful, intelligent, and successful women like us? How the hell did that happen?!*
*Me: I'll tell you how it happened, Jillian. He was very charming at first; he was chivalrous, he spoke intelligently, he cooked great meals for you, entertained your friends, and beguiled your family.*
*Jillian: Yes!*
*Me: Then he would come over to your house for a few hours and pamper you. The next visit he stayed a little longer, then a little longer. Then, he would leave small personal items at your house – a comb, a pair of socks, a few shirts – any reason that he could use to come back over.*
*Jillian: Yes, he did that!*
*Me: Then he started to spend the night, each time bringing a few more items with him, and before you knew it, he was moved in. He was the perfect house guest. He cooked, he cleaned, he removed the trash, cared for the lawn…everything you'd want a man to do for you.*
*Jillian: Oh my God! It's like you were there!*
*Me: But then, you noticed that he was there a little too often for*

*your comfort and you desired some space. And whenever you'd suggest that he go home for the night, he would resist. He'd resist a little at first, but as time went on, his resistance got more aggressive. And by this time, he had keys to your place.*

***Jillian:*** *I can't believe we fell for it.*

***Me:*** *Well, Jillian it's not something to beat ourselves up about. After all, like you said, we're beautiful, intelligent, and successful women. He saw that clearly and immediately put a plan into action that would cause us to put our guard down. We are attracted to men who display chivalry and intelligence. He used that...heavily.*

After that conversation, I found myself wanting to get to know her because I felt we were connected through our traumatic experiences with him. She never gave me her number, and she never called me again. I suspect that she didn't fully feel comfortable befriending me because she just wasn't sure whether or not I could be trusted. Understandable. Still, I felt a sense of longing to help the next woman...to somehow warn her of how manipulative he can be, and how to protect herself. This book is my way of doing that.

In doing this, maybe the "Winstons" of the world will be seen for who they are sooner rather than later. They're not easy to spot. There's no scarlet letter on their forehead to indicate their abusive behavior, so unfortunately we have to actually engage the relationship to make that discovery.

I recall watching a brief video online about a group of women who escaped an abusive partnership. The one thing that stood out the most was a statement one of the ladies said, "No one tells you on the first date, *'Hey, I'm going to start beating you in 6 months.'*" And she's absolutely right! Many abusers are fully aware of their patterns and they know that they can't reveal too much too soon. So the goal is usually to win your trust, then break you down. After all, how easy would it be to leave someone to whom you have no emotional attachment? Fairly easy, right? But what if you've fallen in love? Grown close to their family? Made a connection with their children? And vice versa?

Victims of abuse don't usually want the relationship itself to stop; they want the _abuse_ to stop. They want to continue the romantic aspect of the union without the mistreatment.

So how did _you_ get here? Here are a few explanations; one (or more) may apply to you if you're a survivor or current victim:

1. **Entering a Relationship Vulnerably:** Being in an emotional or mental state of vulnerability increases the chances of entering an abusive relationship because the abuser appears to be a human safe haven – a diversion from that which you wish to escape.
2. **Ignoring Your Instinct:** If you have experienced a series of poor choices, you may begin to question your instinct. So when your gut tells you that this person is bad news, you don't give it as much attention because you're no longer confident in your decision-making process.
3. **Childhood Observations:** Abusive patterns and behaviors that you witnessed as a child subconsciously molded you to gravitate towards mistreatment. If the only thing you've observed is dysfunction, how do you know what a healthy, functional relationship looks like?
4. **Lack of Faith in Yourself:** When you don't trust that you are fully capable of handling life's challenges, it's very easy to seek someone to validate you – which is something that abusers are very good at in the beginning.

5. **Signs Were Ignored:** When the signs of abuse surfaced, you may have chalked them up to your partner "having a bad day," or "just a little edgy today." They seemed little at first, but a series of little things can become one HUGE thing, and you're the one who gets hurt.

6. **Looking for Someone to SAVE:** Many of us are inclined to help people; it's built into our DNA. When we see a "wounded" soul, we caress them and nurture them like a sick puppy and receive massive satisfaction from it because we're "saving" them from themselves, or a mean ol' nasty world. We take great pride in that preverbal cape flapping in the wind behind us.

7. **The Soul Mate Syndrome:** Initial attraction can easily be confused with "finding your soul mate" especially if you're actively seeking it. In your eyes, they can do no wrong because you've found the person you were meant to be with for the rest of your life…or so you thought.

8. **Misguided Belief Systems:** This one is rather sensitive for most people, especially for religious believers. There are faiths that discourage ending a marriage under any circumstances. The belief that "a higher power has brought us together" is enough to feel condemned and sinful if you decide to leave.

I'm quite sure there are many other reasons, but the above list covers a quite a bit. These are interchangeable as well. One can certainly lead to another.

## Falling in Love with Potential

Growing up in the black community, I was inundated with a strong culture of supporting each other no matter what. I subscribed to this idea with everything I had in me. It was all about the "Strong Black Woman" partnered with the "Strong

Black Man." All I wanted to do was help my partner grow and, in turn, I would grow too. It sounds noble and respectable, but sometimes it got me into trouble because I would always see what he _could do_ as opposed to what he was _actually doing._ If he portrayed the image of a promising successful black man, I was all in. I wanted to be his "ride or die" chick. I wanted to be the one he would look to in times of dejection to seek solace. This filled me with a great sense of pride – not to mention a grounded sense of community.

But the downside to falling in love with people's potential is that at some point you realize that that's all there is...just potential. Sure, you can see them building a business, growing a company, or inventing an innovative product or service. But after a significant amount of time passes without any tangible results, you begin to wonder if _they_ can see it; or see it to the extent that you do.

Potential is what kept me in relationships long after its expiration date. So I lost patience with them because they weren't producing at a pace that I believed they should and eventually decided to leave. And although I ended those relationships, they still permanently held captive a piece of me that I couldn't get back. In abusive situations, the person's potential can keep you engaged far beyond the time to leave.

**Historical Effect**
There's a place that holds evidence of some logical reasoning surrounding present day behaviors...it's called the past. Many people don't consider the connection between their historical lineage and their present day circumstances. This can leave you feeling as if everything that's happening right now is your fault. If you haven't made this connection, let's look at some cultural

historical accounts to see if we can attach it to some of the current situations. I'm outlining three communities – Black, Hispanic/Latino, and LGBTQA. If your lineage isn't represented here, I do encourage researching it on your own and following the same process.

**Path to Recovery Model**
To offer some insight, we're going to be using the model below.

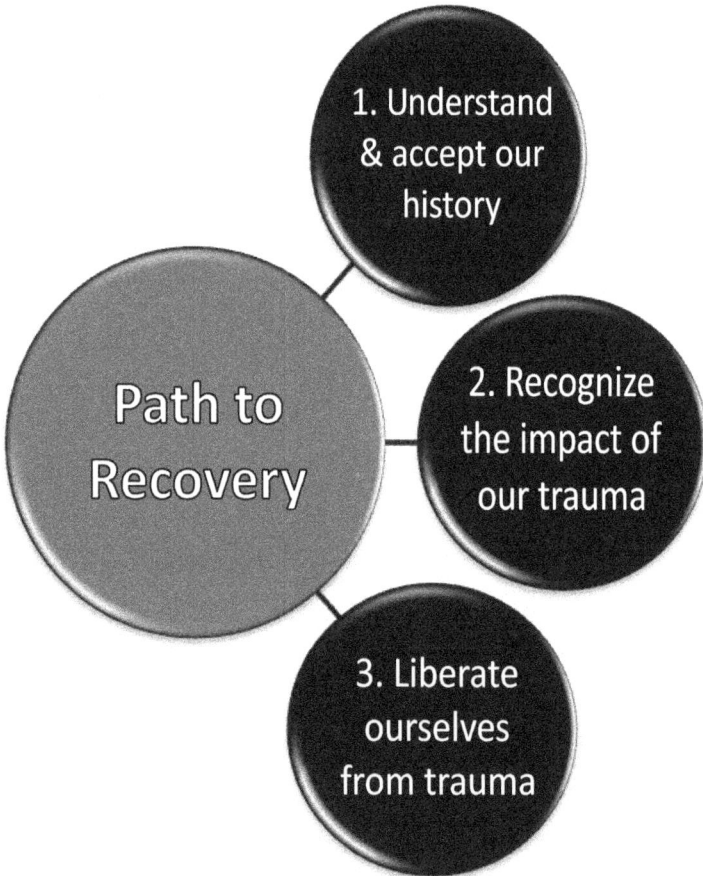

## 1. Understand & accept our history
### Black/African-American:

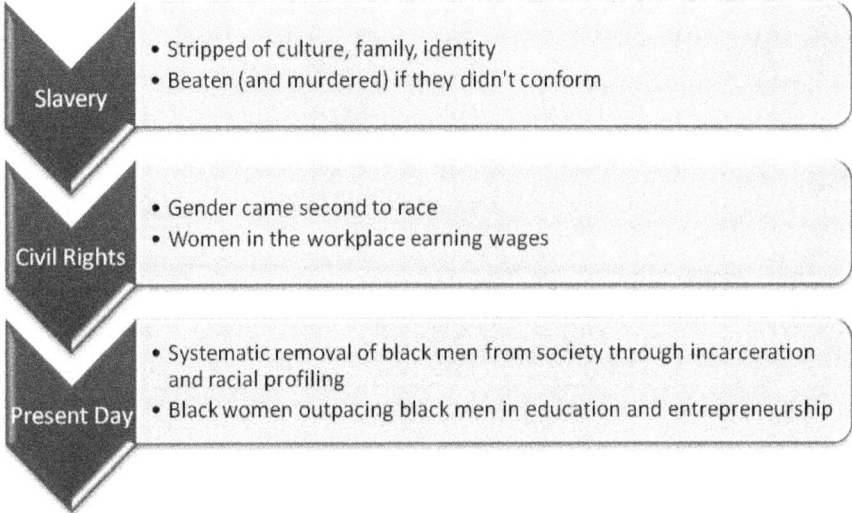

**Slavery**
- Stripped of culture, family, identity
- Beaten (and murdered) if they didn't conform

**Civil Rights**
- Gender came second to race
- Women in the workplace earning wages

**Present Day**
- Systematic removal of black men from society through incarceration and racial profiling
- Black women outpacing black men in education and entrepreneurship

### Hispanic/Latino:

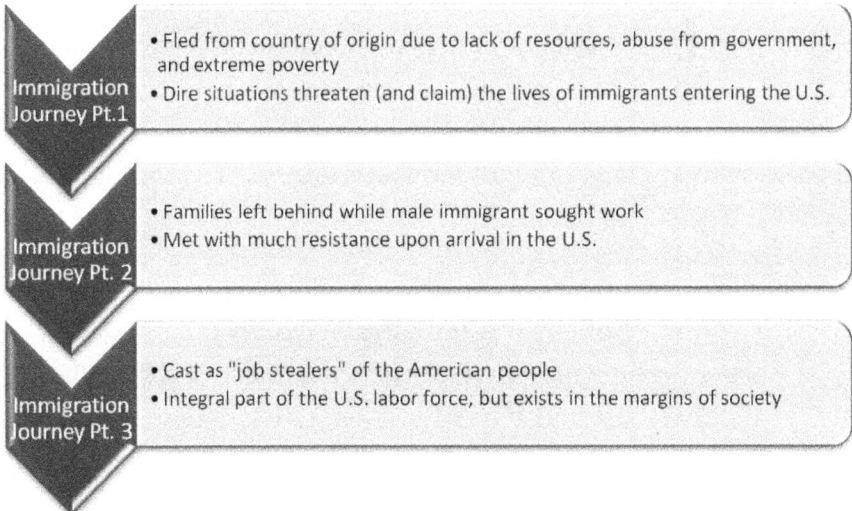

**Immigration Journey Pt.1**
- Fled from country of origin due to lack of resources, abuse from government, and extreme poverty
- Dire situations threaten (and claim) the lives of immigrants entering the U.S.

**Immigration Journey Pt. 2**
- Families left behind while male immigrant sought work
- Met with much resistance upon arrival in the U.S.

**Immigration Journey Pt. 3**
- Cast as "job stealers" of the American people
- Integral part of the U.S. labor force, but exists in the margins of society

LGBTQA:

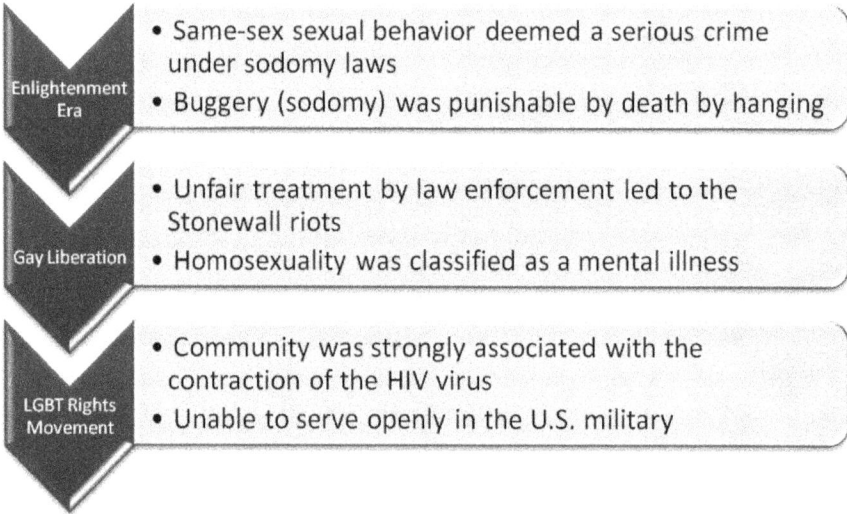

- Enlightenment Era
  - Same-sex sexual behavior deemed a serious crime under sodomy laws
  - Buggery (sodomy) was punishable by death by hanging

- Gay Liberation
  - Unfair treatment by law enforcement led to the Stonewall riots
  - Homosexuality was classified as a mental illness

- LGBT Rights Movement
  - Community was strongly associated with the contraction of the HIV virus
  - Unable to serve openly in the U.S. military

I also want to point out that in addition to your historical lineage, you want to review your **personal** history as well. Think of all of the traumatic experiences that you have faced. Perhaps you were a victim of child molestation, had alcoholic parents, grew up without much money or food, or witnessed a horrific sene that has haunted you periodically. All of these things impact your life in ways that you may not have considered.

2. **Recognize the impact of our trauma**
   The impact of our trauma can seem invisible to those who are experiencing it. Historical trauma can have similar effects in present day situations across many ethnicities. Below is a list of common responses to historical trauma. Review them to see if you can make a connection to your current situation:

- o Grieving the loss of intimacy
- o Depression
- o Attempts to numb the pain [alcohol, gambling, binge eating, energy drinks, drugs...etc]
- o Suicidal ideation & gestures
- o Fixation to the trauma [*"I'm a victim, and I can't let it go."*]
- o Survivor guilt – "Ancestors went through trauma, and I didn't." [Also, surviving military soldiers experience this when they come back home.]
- o Psychic numbing - The condition brought on by trauma resulting in incapacity to express emotions such as love or closeness.
- o Loyalty to ancestral suffering and the deceased. You identify your existence through the suffering of your ancestors. Thus, having the mentality that you are supposed to suffer and sacrifice.
- o Idealizing how life should be as opposed to the way it really is (Also referred to as 'Compensatory Fantasies')
- o Vitality in our own life is seen as a betrayal to ancestors who suffered so much (Similar to survivor guilt)
- o Impaired parenting
- o Attachment failure – You're unable to get emotionally attached to anyone.
- o Delayed traumatic triggers – For example, if we look at a group of people who survived a mass shooting, and a few days later they were in a parking lot when a car backfired *loudly.* They may respond as if the shooting is happening all over again. The experience was REAL for them, even though there wasn't a definite threat present.

Furthermore, many of the lessons that our parents, guardians, and other caregivers taught us during our formative years play a heavy role in how we view ourselves, the outside world, and the people in it. Let's take a look at some "lessons" you may have been taught and how they have impacted you today.

Lesson: *"If you can't say something nice, don't say anything at all."*

> This teaches us to supress our natural desire to communicate our need to be understood, safe, and whole. Babies cry instinctively when something's bothering them and parents intuitively come to the aid of that child to solve the issue. Somewhere along the line, that child is taught to forego their need to express themselves as opposed to being taught *how* to communicate that need effectively.

Lesson: *"Eat everything on your plate."*

> When you're in a household that has very little food, it can seem like a waste when food goes uneaten. The underlying message that our parents were trying to teach us is not to be wasteful and to appreciate the fact that we have food to eat. The challenge with this tactic is that it trains us to eat even after the point of feeling full. Is there any wonder why many Americans are obese?

Lesson: *"If he hits you, it's because he likes you."*

> This one in particular really gets under my skin. When a child comes home from school to inform their parents that someone has physically hurt them (which is what they're taught to do), and the parent offers the reasoning, "...because they like you." It undoubtedly confuses the child. Now consider this – a 5 year old girl was smacked in the head by a little boy at school, informed her parents

that she's been hurt, then told that it's because she is liked, ***how does that affect the way she views relationships when she gets older?*** If she is being physically abused by her partner, somewhere deep in her psyche is the thought process, "It's only because they like you."

3. **Liberate ourselves from trauma**

   Liberation can't happen without first knowing that we need to be liberated. The process of liberation begins with intentionally releasing what we have learned and being open to discovering our own personal truths even if it means losing close relationships that have been a part of our lives for many years. It can be frightening and uncomfortable, but oppositely it can make you feel free and emancipated. Let's get you started with a few steps:

o <u>Release the ego</u> – Forget what you thought you knew about life. Humble yourself to let go of the need to control every aspect of your life. Understand that you cannot rule the actions of others, just yours.

o <u>Dump old habits</u> – Those self deprecating tendencies that held you captive no longer serve you well, so walk away from them. You do this by replacing them with new behaviors that better serve your desire to be liberated.

o <u>Live right now</u> – It's more than a challenge to live in the present when there are so many details of future projects consuming our minds. When you find your mind drifting too far into the future [or the past], consciously bring your awareness to the present moment and focus on what it is that you need right now.

It is my hope that reviewing the historical context of your personal and ancestral memoirs has shed some liberating light on how you may have landed in your current abusive situation. With this in mind, you're now perfectly positioned to alter the course of your life permanently.

How Did I Get Here?

# Why Do People Stay?

4

In the first chapter, we covered one of the myths surrounding IPV – "Victims of abuse can just leave." According to the U.S. Department of Justice, the most dangerous time for a victim is when he/she tries to leave. There are many reasons why victims remain in the relationship: economic dependence, lack of support systems, and previous attempts to leave that ended in severe abuse [to name a few]. Abuse can increase as much as 70% when the abuser feels that he/she is losing control of the victim. So the victim stays to avoid abuse that could potentially lead to death.

I find it interesting and somewhat appalling to hear others say things like, "She/He obviously likes it, otherwise they would just leave." Or, "Look, they created this situation so I don't feel anything for them." Here's what many people simply don't understand - Abuse does not happen immediately. In fact, the signs of abuse don't usually appear until sometime after the partners have fallen in love.

When speaking to men and women about whether or not they believe they'll ever be in an abusive relationship, the most common response is, "No! I'd just leave!" When I asked why they felt so strongly about it, many of them responded with "I'm too" statements:

- o I'm too independent
- o I'm too smart
- o I'm too confident
- o I'm too wealthy
- o I'm too aware
- o I'm too streetwise
- o I'm too educated

- o I'm too tough
- o I'm too intolerant

What I later realized is that some of them were in fact committed to an abuser at some point in their lives, but simply didn't recognize it as abusive.

**Abuse Wears a Mask**

In chapter 2, we outlined the varying degrees of abuse. Some of which you may not have realized were actually abuse. The very same people who made the "I'm too" statements later revealed why they were "too smart, savvy, independent...etc" to be abused. It was because they've had experiences in previous relationships that made them a little more discerning. However, in those previous relationships, were textbook signs of various forms of abuse. These are real stories from some of these women:

Yolanda* stated that she couldn't see herself in a relationship with an abuser because she used to date a guy who was angry all the time and she'd never let it get too far. "At first I thought he was just blowing off steam. You know, trying to deal with life the best he could. But then it just started feeling as if he was doing it on purpose." He used to say things to her like, "You're really dumb to be so smart." Yolanda stated that she was in that relationship for about 18 months. She experienced a hostile tone and intense delivery of his messages for 18 months. This is **Verbal Abuse.**

Gina* had a similar story. She stated that she was married to a police officer for 19 years and he had multiple affairs which made her feel poorly about herself. He stopped showing physical, non-sexual affection. She gained significant weight and was frequently on the receiving end of how unattractive she was to him. Despite how many compliments she received from men outside of her marriage, the comments made to her as well as the actions of her husband sent her into a deep depression. "Once, he even [over] complimented another woman right in front of me at a gala. When I told him how that made me feel, he told me I was over reacting." Her relationship entailed malicious withdrawal of affection, ignoring her feelings, and public humiliation. This is a classic case of **Emotional Abuse.**

Dani* had a Cinderella story, or so she thought. She dated a man for 11 years who was very wealthy and generous with his money towards her. She could go shopping, take a vacation, volunteer, and all sorts of things that people couldn't do because of lack of financial resources. She put off going to school because he felt that the lifestyle he created for her was the whole reason she wanted to acquire higher education and that it's no longer necessary. He also discouraged her from going to work. When things started to get shaky in the relationship, he began to withdraw some of the financial freedoms. Eventually, it had gotten to a point where Dani had to ask for everything that she wanted and needed. By this time, she was 100% dependent on him and he knew it. Dani experienced a situation that rendered her 100% dependent on him and coercion from getting a job and pursuing education. These are textbook signs of **Economic Abuse.**

When I ask the question, "How do you know that you've never been in an abusive relationship?" The most common response is, "Because he/she never laid a hand on me." After educating them on the implications of abuse, and identifying those very same signs in their previous relationships, you could see a shift in their demeanor. Some got defensive; others shriveled in their seats. As previously stated, the general public views abuse as physical, and understandably so. The cases of abuse that we see in the mainstream media usually involve some type of physical trauma that has turned fatal.

So to put things into perspective, we'll cover some of the many reasons why victims remain in abusive relationships:

**Love**
Remember, the abuser is someone who has shown love and affection to the point where the victim now cares for them deeply. The sense of commitment to the relationship has an extremely high priority in the victim's life. They can see the "potential" in the abuser and they want the *abuse* to stop, not the relationship. Also, the period of positive affection and love following an abusive episode makes it especially difficult to leave. The abuser may also be the parent of the children involved and the thought of splitting the family is too painful to consider.

**Fear of**
- o Physical harm to themselves and/or their children
- o Doing emotional damage to the children if they lost a parent
- o Not being taken seriously by law enforcement
- o Losing custody of children
- o Friends and family being put in harm's way
- o Going through the legal/court process
- o Being seen as a weak victim
- o Not having a safe place to live

**Lack of Self Confidence/Self Esteem**
This plagues even the best of us at some point or another. But it's even more challenging to end a relationship when your abuser

has systematically trickled insults that destroy what little self worth you started with. The belief that you simply cannot do better than the partner you currently have reigns so prevalently for many victims, that it literally stops them from seeking a partnership elsewhere. Abusers find it relatively easy to further diminish the perceived value of their victims when they enter the relationship with very little at all.

## Cultural Pressures

Many cultures heavily frown upon divorce or any other means of breaking up a family and thus creating an enormous strain on the victim if she/he wants out of the relationship. Possible consequences include being shamed, and even being banned from the family. Typically, these cultures have strong patriarchal norms, which don't give women much power and authority. So the thought of rebelling against such customs is a very frightful experience. She may also feel like there's no way out, as the family and its traditions is the only thing she's known her entire life.

## Economic Dependency

If the abuser has been the primary bread winner in the relationship, the victim does not likely have access to the funds needed to make a departure from the relationship. If the victim has relied on the abuser for every human need – food, shelter, clothing, personal items, transportation, and everyday maintenance – then the victim feels as if there's no other option for them to thrive on their own. Maybe s/he doesn't feel like they have the capacity or skills needed to begin earning money on their own so complacency becomes the norm.

## Unaware of Where to Find Help

If you have never found yourself in an abusive situation before, how could you know what help is available? Even if you are aware that there may be some form of help, many victims don't know where to look safely. Using the computer at home or cell phone can be a deadly act if the abuser discovers that the victim is seeking to get out of the relationship. What about telling a friend? The victim may refrain from sharing their experience(s) with others out of fear of being judged, or because they fear that involving another person could put them in danger.

There are far too many variables in individual relationships to list all of the reasons why people stay. But understand this – just because someone remains in abuse does not mean that they aren't seeking a way out.

If You Leave, I Will Kill You!

# Reclaiming Your Strength

5

To activate the launch sequence that gets you out of abuse, it's essential to reclaim your strength. Some of you may believe that you simply have none, but I beg to differ. Consider this – the years that you spent enduring the abuse, apologizing for things that weren't your fault, minimizing your desires & goals, catering to the needs of your abuser, all while keeping the family together, takes more strength than any human can conjure up consciously. You just did it because you felt that that's what was needed to move your life forward. So the first step to reclaiming your strength is to recognize that you have it.

**No More Apologizing**
What do you have to be sorry for? Why should you sacrifice one more degree of energy for someone whose only desire is to control you? It's almost instinctive to apologize when your abuser displays their disapproval of your behavior or choices. Many victims apologize without even knowing what it is that they've done in the first place. At the first sign of conflict, "I'm sorry" comes flying from their lips faster than they can hold them; anything to avoid a fight or some form of punishment. If you're someone who has endured abuse for a long period of time, then apologizing may seem like a natural occurrence. No more. Do not apologize for:

1. Your appearance
2. Being smart
3. Shedding tears
4. Asserting yourself
5. Offering your opinion
6. Using your best judgment
7. Protecting your family
8. Disrupting the status quo
9. Breaking rules that were designed to oppress you

10. Setting boundaries
11. Being in disagreement with someone
12. Asking for what you need
13. Not knowing something
14. Your values
15. Your income
16. Being your authentic self
17. Wanting to be alone
18. The desire to eat
19. Occasional absentmindedness
20. Wanting to leave a relationship

The truth is that when you over-apologize, it gives a very weak and uncertain impression. This makes you an easy target for manipulation. But when you are unapologetic about who you are, those around you will do one of two things – roll **with** you, or get rolled **over.**

**Use Envy to Your Advantage**
I'm sure you've been told that envy is a bad thing; that it causes you to take actions that do harm to another person. Envy does not do this, jealously does.

What's the difference between envy and jealousy? Envy is a signal that appears when you recognize that there's something that you would like to have or experience in your life. It may not have been something that you've ever noticed before. Perhaps you drive by a house that exemplifies the home that you've always dreamed of as a child. Or maybe you see a couple taking skiing lessons together and you admire their willingness to learn as a couple.

Jealousy is something that makes you wish that no one else has what it is that you want. So much so, that you're willing to take action to remove that element from another's life. Jealously, when unleashed, can be dangerous and even deadly.

Some years ago, I was introduced to a woman who was scheduled to interview me for a publication. After a series of questions related to my work, we ended the interview. Upon completion, she sarcastically made the statement, "It must be nice being able to wake up whenever you feel like it instead of to an alarm clock like the rest of us." I received that statement and translated it back to her, "You're saying that given the opportunity, you would choose to do your job on your own schedule instead of someone else's." To which she responded, "Hell yeah! In a heartbeat." She didn't want <u>my</u> career; she simply desired the flexibility that my career offered me. *This is envy.*

When an abuser decides that s/he will kill their victim rather than see them with anyone else, *this is jealously.*

So how do you use envy to your advantage? When you recognize something that you want but don't yet have, use that desire to build towards obtaining it. Perhaps even asking the person or organization that currently has what you want how to secure it is a great way to start. Like I stated before, sometimes you don't realize what you want until to see it.

**Build Strategic Alliances**
In other words, you want to create a team of allies who will support you in your efforts to leave your abusive relationship. They can be found in many places – Shelters, hotlines, online support groups, and even your own family.

This transition is difficult enough on your own, so why not make it less burdensome by calling on those who have a desire to help? You can learn about how others have escaped their abuser(s), share your story, find safety for you and your children, and feel less alone in your journey.

In doing research for this book, I interviewed countless men and women to hear their tragic stories. It's my hope that their advice offers you inspiration that will help you reclaim the strength you need to change your abusive situation. My outline was fairly simple:

- o Were you Married, Domestic Partners, or Boyfriend/Girlfriend?
- o Did you live together during the abuse?
- o How long you were together?
- o How long into the relationship did the abuse start?
- o Did you see any signs?
- o If yes, what were they?
- o Did you tell anybody you were being abused?
- o If so, did they try to help you?
- o Did you continue the relationship with them after that?
- o If so, why?
- o How did you get away from that situation?
- o Have you seen him/her since the abuse?
- o If so, why?
- o Where do you go for help?
- o If you were sitting in a room full of young girls, boys, men, and women, what would you want to say to them about Domestic Violence?

I'm going to focus on the last question because I believe it brings home the point of this book. In listening to the answers, I compiled a list that I believe should be used as pillars upon which your very existence should stand.

**Katherine\* says**: Know that you are not powerless. You must be stronger than you imagine you can be. The person who is actually afraid is the abuser; they're deathly afraid of losing control over you. And since you're the one who decides whether or not that happens, the power then shifts to you.

**Dahlia\* advises**: Be aware of the warning signs. You will have a tendency to dismiss them. If it starts to escalate don't let them know your plan to leave. Love yourself. If they hit you, that's not love.

**Regan\* says**: You're beautiful children of God. Ask God to show how you look through His eyes. I used to call myself a "dumb shit" and the voice said, "How can you call yourself that if you're filled with ME?" Don't let anyone's opinion determine your value or worth.

**Don\* says:** It's NOT okay to be abused. Don't assume that it's normal behavior, because it's not. Recognize the signs. People confuse control with love. CONTROLLING BEHAVIOR IS NOT LOVE. Have more confidence in yourself to reject that behavior. It can cost you your life.

**Cameron\* says:** Value yourself. Have a great relationship with yourself. If you do that, you will not entertain a relationship of abuse. You'll see it. Talk to your children before they become 18 and ask them, "What do you like about you?" Tell them what a healthy relationship looks like. Being single is not a curse, it's a blessing.

**Betty\* advises:** Check in with yourself from time to time. Ask yourself if you're genuinely happy. If the answer is no, then take inventory of what [and who] is in your life and start making changes immediately. You'll find that if you keep doing this, you will notice a pattern of things that you're happy about as well as things that you don't like.

**Sam\* says:** Set a healthy example for your children. Let them know what a loving relationship looks like. Comfort them at night before they go to bed, then pray and comfort yourself too. The answers will come and when they do, have _faith_ that you're strong enough to bring you and your kids out of that ordeal.

**Veronica\* advises:** Stop calling yourself a victim. You will start to behave like one. Instead, refer to yourself as a vicTOR and your behavior will follow suit.

**Traci\* asks:** What do you have to lose by staying in that kind of relationship? Your life, that's what. What is your life worth to you? If it's priceless, protect it as such.

**Quiana\* says:** If your children tell you that they're being abused, listen to them. There's nothing worse than a child having the courage to tell someone they're being touched inappropriately, then being reprimanded for it. Your child will lose faith in all that's supposed to be there to protect them. So be their protector, damnit!!

**Helen\* declares:** This was tough to admit, but all of the abuse laid on my shoulders because I allowed the behavior for so long. Even in the beginning, I knew that I should have spoken up, but I didn't because I didn't want to be alone. So to you I say – If you allowed it, then you can stop it. It's gonna be the scariest thing you'll ever do, but you gotta do it in order to be free.

**Freda\* says:** If you have to disappear from your friends and family to get rid of [him], then do it. It may be lonely, but think about how lonely you already were in your relationship. Don't feel pressure to tell your family everything. Take time to get yourself together before you face anybody else.

The strength that you need is already inside of you. Call it forth. If you need more incentive, think about your children, your personal safety, and the bright future that awaits you when you break free. You've been held prisoner long enough.

# Exit Strategies

6

There are ways to leave a relationship once you have decided that you will no longer tolerate the loathsome behavior from your abuser. So when that happens, it's time to _plan_ your escape. I say "plan" your escape because although victims would like very much to simply leave, it's not always a wise decision if you're not fully prepared.

Maria* decided she was going to leave her abuser one night after the biggest physical fight they'd ever had. She packed a bag and told him it was over. Upon seeing and hearing this, her abuser fell into an even deeper fit of rage and nearly beat her to death. Maria now has permanent hearing loss and a slightly disfigured face because of that beating.

One of the most important things to remember when planning an exit strategy is to _not allow your standard behavior and routine to change in any way_. This will arouse suspicion and it will completely defeat the purpose of escaping the abuse as unscathed as possible. Also, this book will likely fall into the hands of abusers as well, looking for clues as to when their victim may choose to leave. If your routine doesn't change, it makes it more difficult to decipher your escape plan.

Derek* chose to leave in the middle of the night while his abuser slept. When Derek shifted to get out of bed, his abuser awakened and asked what he was doing to which Derek replied, "I can't sleep, so I'm just going to go for a drive." Derek has never done this before, and it set off a red flag. The abuser immediately reached for the gun that he kept in the night stand drawer and threatened to kill Derek if he set foot outside of the bedroom. Scared to death, Derek complied and from that point forward, his abuser monitored his every move with relentless scrutiny.

Also, I strongly advise against going to friends and family member's homes that are familiar to your abuser. While in the relationship, if your abuser has visited your loved ones with you, they will instinctively look for you there. Many abusers don't care about hurting anyone who stands in the way of getting to you, so if at all possible, avoid putting them in that position.

Planning an escape requires foresight and an ability to operate under pressure. This is because if there comes a point when you have to set the plan in motion hurriedly and under duress, you can do so without compromising the safety of your family and friends.

Some escape plans require some time to cultivate, and others happen more quickly depending on the severity of the situation. Here I am going to list some ideas and strategies to plan your escape and you decide which one(s) work for you. The purpose is to provide you with some options so you don't feel trapped and hopeless; they're to give you some freedom to start over if you so choose. You may opt to implement many of the below options, or perhaps just one will suffice...you decide. Let's get to it!

**Exit Strategies**

1. Purchase a prepaid cell phone, or apply for a free government cell phone. Program all pertinent contacts into the new phone including shelters and food banks. Then hide the cell phone (and its charger) in a safe deposit box at a bank, or a storage facility. When you're ready to escape, leave your regular cell phone behind or at home with the abuser. Before doing so, reset the phone to the factory default to get rid of all contacts and call

history. Also remove the SIM card and micro SD card. The reason for leaving the phone behind is so you cannot be tracked just in case a tracking device or location app has been placed on it (that happened to me once).

2.  Purchase a bus, plane, or train ticket to anywhere right away [for your children as well if applicable]. Although you will not take the trip, you will have a credit towards a future trip. Be sure to use a method of payment that cannot be traced such as prepaid debit card or use cash at the counter. For example, purchase a train ticket from Chicago to Orlando (the dates don't matter). Call the train carrier to let them know that you will not be able to take the trip to receive a credit with that carrier. When you are ready to escape, you will have means to do so even if you're flat broke.

3.  Designate a "safe place" with someone you trust. This is a place you agree to go to when you're in trouble and need help. Again, do not go to a loved one's home or place of business. Example: Theresa and Bob are friends. Theresa tells Bob that she plans to escape and may not be in a position to say when it will happen. When Theresa leaves and her abuser calls around to ask about her whereabouts, Bob then knows where she likely is. Bob goes to the "safe place" to pick her up and take her to a safer destination.

4.  Use code words to signal distress. When texting, emailing, tweeting, or posting on Facebook, you can use this method to communicate distress to those whom you trust. For example, the word "hilarious" can mean *I'm*

*leaving and I will be in touch soon.* Or using some type of punctuation excessively can be a code as well. Using "..." can mean *my abuser is here.* So if Sheila felt she was in danger and decided that she was going to leave, she may text her trusted friend, "Girl...I just heard a joke and it was hilarious!" The friend understands that that means, "My abuser is here and I'm leaving. I will be in touch soon." *Please do not use the code words I just provided*. As I stated before, this book will land in the hands of abusers as well, so create your own list of code words and distress signals. This way, you can communicate your plans and/or current situation without making it obvious.

5. Go to the library to research escape plans. If you have a shared computer at home, or one that your abuser has access to, do not use it to look up shelter locations, food banks, hotels, or car rentals. Instead, use a public computer during a time when your abuser cannot be with you. Public libraries delete browsing history nightly to keep the machines operating at peak performance. If you choose to print the information, *do not bring it home!* Instead, take it directly to a bank's safe deposit box or storage unit. Don't leave it in the car either. Put it in a place that requires some form of security to access.

6. Store necessary medications in a safe place that you can access later. If you're on any medications, have extra in your safe deposit box, locker, or storage unit so you can stay healthy when you escape. Rita* had to take meds for her high blood pressure daily and when she decided to escape, she had to leave in a hurry and left her meds behind. She wasn't in a position to get more, and her

blood pressure reached dangerous levels and she was admitted to a hospital. Her medical records indicated that her abuser was her emergency contact, so when the hospital reached out to him, you can imagine his rage when he discovered what she was up to.

7. Order duplicates of your birth certificate, driver's license, passport, and social security card. Have those stored in a safe place as well. My ex abuser destroyed all of my identification and you cannot imagine how difficult it is to get it back without anything to prove you are who you say you are. I went to the department of motor vehicles and they said I needed a birth certificate and social security card. I went to the courthouse to get a birth certificate and I was told that I needed a photo ID. I went to the social security office, and they required the same thing. I even had a police report explaining that my identification had gotten destroyed, and it wasn't enough. So, with my back against the wall, I created a phony work ID and I took it to the courthouse to obtain my birth certificate, and from there I was able to get the rest.

8. Do not use any form of currency that is associated with the abuser. Any checks, debit or credit card(s) that you share or that he/she has access to should not be used! This includes online accounts such as PayPal. It's much too easy to go online or call the customer service representative to track where purchases are being made. Pay in cash, or put the money on a prepaid debit card, which can be purchased from a local retailer like Walgreens or even gas stations. They don't have any of your personal information linked to it.

9. Delete your social media accounts altogether. You need to be "off the radar" for a while. Your abuser will certainly try to track you down using your social media accounts and friends associated with those accounts. In addition, many sites will literally showcase the location of where you posted. Diane* decided to simply remove the location feature and delete all friends associated with her ex from her Facebook account.   One of her associates (not knowing Diane's situation), commented on a recent photo stating, "I recognize that place! I grew up down the street from there in _____." The comment was made public and Diane's location was disclosed.

10. Consider placing a security freeze on your credit reports. This will prevent anyone from viewing it without your written authorization. Abusers may want to pull your credit to see if any new accounts have been opened, or if you have obtained a new job. Consider this option especially if you and the abuser have lived together for a while and have access to a lot of your personal information.

11. Change the passwords on all of your email accounts. Make sure to change them to something completely unrelated to a commonality between you and your abuser.

12. Request a security PIN for all of your utility, cell phone, and new banking accounts. Because your abuser will likely know the last four digits of your social security number, change the security feature to require a custom PIN that you have designated.

13. Remove your abuser from all insurance accounts; this includes beneficiary benefits.

14. Download a safety app on your phone. It's designed to alert your support system when you are in trouble. Circle of 6 and PFO Shield are highly recommended.

15. Have an escape kit stored in a storage facility. There are many items you can include in your kit. Canned goods are a safe bet, bottles of water, extra clothes for you and the kids, toiletry items, cell phone charger and any meds. Be sure to pack two can openers and disposable cutlery as well.

Having a plan makes it easier to escape your abuser unscathed. You feel more confident in yourself, and you're not as fearful. Hopefully the above mentioned tactics will assist you in creating a plan that works best for you. Remember to keep these things to yourself, or reveal them to only people whom you trust with your life and safety. Godspeed!

# Exit Strategies

# Staying Off the Beaten Path

7

Leaving an abuser is extremely difficult when you love them. And the thought of leaving is scary for a number of reasons; one of the strongest is being alone. But the fear of leaving sometimes pales in comparison to the fear of what you're going to do once you're actually gone. In many cases, the abuser has been the primary source of basic life needs: food, shelter, money, clothing, insurance, and transportation. This is all to control you, see?

Once you're out of an abusive relationship, you say to yourself that it will never happen again. Unfortunately, many victims return to the abuser or other relationships that closely resemble the previous abuse.

After successfully implementing your exit strategy and you escape the beaten path, it's important that you form new habits to stay off of the beaten path. How do you do that? I'm offering some suggestions, and perhaps they will resonate with you. Being pro-active in your self development significantly reduces the chances of returning to abusive relationships.

**For Your Wallet**
If you're someone who relied on your abuser to financially support you, it's a challenge to now care for yourself [and your children]. You may have to get creative in terms of how to earn money. Here are some imaginative ways to earn some cash legally and quickly:

- Drive! – If you have a clean driving record, your own car, and can pass a criminal background check, you may want to consider driving others around for money. There are several companies who pay drivers to pick up and drop off people in your city. They go through measures to increase the safety of the driver like confirming the identity of the passengers, taking their photos, and tracking your location while working so they know where you are. Some companies include: Uber, Lyft, and Sidecar.

o <u>Get Micro-Funded</u> – If you have a skill or a special quirk, you can get paid to showcase it! Online communities such as Fiverr.com allows you to get paid doing what you already know how to do. For example, if you know how to convert documents from one format to another, write press releases, offer marketing advice, create videos, translate, Photoshop pictures, blog, or do voiceovers, then this is the place for you! You get paid $5 every time someone orders your gig. And you even have the option of charging more for additional features like extra fast delivery. Fiverr.com takes $1, leaving you with $4 per gig with the basic fee. There are many people around the world making a living on Fiverr.com. There's literally hundreds of thousands of gigs posted and you can be one of them. I even saw someone who could draw your picture on a grain of rice. So get creative!

o <u>Walk the dog</u> – Start a dog-walking service.

o <u>House Sit</u> – Use online services to get approved such as MindMyHouse.com or HouseSittersAmerica.com

o <u>Get Handy in the Yard</u> – Offer to mow the lawns, rake the leaves, and shovel snow for your neighbors and build a clientele. This is one of the methods that I used when I lived in a shelter to make some cash fast.

o <u>Start a home-based business</u> – If you're already skilled at something, turn it into a business. Take inventory of your skills and see if you can make money from it. Can you cook? Dance? Fix computers? Clean houses? Repair household things? Sew? Braid hair? Give fashion advice?

When I had a life coaching business, one of my clients told me that she was so inspired by the movie *The Pursuit of Happiness*, that she approached a woman on the street whom she perceived to be financially well-off and offered to be her personal assistant. The woman didn't need one, but noticed how well dressed my client was and instead asked her to be a personal shopper. Why wait for opportunity? Create it!

It's all about having options and multiple streams of income. Empowering yourself financially gives you a sense of accomplishment and self sufficiency, so you're less likely to seek another to provide that for you.

**For Your Heart**
Fulfilling your heart is extremely important when permanently removing yourself from abusive relationships. This doesn't necessarily refer to romantic matters of the heart, but feeding the heart of humankind which, in turn, feeds you. Here are some ways to contribute:

- Volunteer – Offer your time to domestic violence shelters. This can be a bit tricky because emotionally you may still be very raw from your personal experience, so tread lightly at first. You may also choose to share your story with the victims to offer them some support.
- Join an Online Empowerment Group – You can join a community of people who specialize in personal growth & development. MeetUp.com is an excellent resource to find local groups who meet regularly for a very specific thing. You can type in keywords like "Abuse Support, Domestic Violence, Life After Abuse…" to find local groups in your area. You don't have to choose groups associated with DV either. You can search groups who gather for

things that you enjoy like pottery, dancing, writing, or yoga. The point is to locate a group of people who gather to do things that fulfill your heart.

- o <u>Attend Events That Empower You</u> – It's fantastic to gather in intimate groups, but don't forget the live events that are designed to enhance your personal growth. You can search for such events on Eventbrite.com, AllConferences.com, or simply do an internet search. It's an excellent way to bond with new people and receive new resources to contribute back to the world.

## For Your Spirit

You may be religious, spiritual, or identify some other kind of way, but feeding the soul is imperative to staying away from abuse.

- o <u>Attend Church Services</u> – If you were once a church-goer, return and see if it still resonates with you.
- o <u>Read Spiritual Books</u> – This may be the Bible, The Holy Quran [or Koran], or other inspirational books. Even when you're driving, you can listen to audio books to further enhance the spiritual reconnection.
- o <u>Daily Mantra</u> – Develop a habit that feeds your spirit on a daily basis. This could be something in depth such meditating for an hour, or something simple such as reciting a prayer when you wake up. This creates a focal point for the day – a foundation upon which the rest of the day will stand. How do you go about learning how to meditate or locating a prayer that resonates with you? There's an app for that! I downloaded an app called Buddhist Meditation on my cell phone and it helps keep me centered, even though I don't identify as a Buddhist. Whatever works for you...do it!

**For Your Body**

The vessel that you carry around was designed to heal itself. A healthy body leads to clear thoughts, processes, and execution. When you physically feel good, it trickles into other aspects of your life. Let's start taking better care of it.

- o Take a Self Defense Class – This works on many levels. Not only are you learning how to protect yourself from physical dangers, but you're strengthening your body. There's a higher degree of self confidence that comes along with knowing how to protect yourself as well.

  I can recall going to pick up a friend from a Kuk Sool class and I arrived early. I walked in, sat on the bench and watched the others. The instructor looked over at me and said, "Hit the mat." I chuckled because I thought it was funny and soon realized that he was not joking. He said, "No one observes in my class. You join us or wait outside." I stood to my feet very nervous about what was going to happen. All of the students in the class stared at me as I walked to the middle of the room and removed my shoes. For the next 40 minutes, I was taught how to counter-attack if someone tried to choke me. I learned how to break fingers, bring my attacker to his knees, and how to crush an esophagus. It was scary, physically grueling, and somehow liberating at the same time. Then he said something to me that will forever be burned into my memory, "You never know when you'll be in a situation when **your** life and someone else's has to end through violence. At least now, _you_ get to make that decision."

  That's the advice I'm sharing with you. There's a sense of

peace associated with knowing that you have the capacity to really hurt another person if they tried to bring harm to you. You're more likely to walk away because you understand that you don't _have_ to fight if you don't want to.

o Replenish Nutrients – Taking vitamins in the form of pills or liquid helps keep your bodies performing at its best. Expert health professionals will include that the best vitamin should come directly from its natural source...raw foods. Perhaps that route is a bit extreme for you; still make room in your schedule and budget to invest in your body. As you get older, your body doesn't "bounce back" the way it used to, so give it a hand.

**Invite Your Brain**

Immerse yourself in the idea that you are the most powerful, creative, and prevailing creature who ever walked the Earth. Know that you are in complete control of your actions and reactions. Position yourself as a wise decision-maker. You can certainly give your heart to a relationship, but take your brain with you [and use it].

I was in a relationship with a man whom I loved more than I can possibly articulate. But despite how much I loved him, I knew we were not good for one another. Our governing values were not in alignment, and I couldn't see myself spending my non-refundable time defending my every decision, or presenting a watered-down version of my true self to satisfy him. I was very saddened by the fact that it wouldn't likely work out. But I chose to feel grateful to know that I had the capacity to love someone so much. My heart was in 100%, but when I brought my brain with it, I was able to save myself [and him] some unnecessary heartache.

**Don't Look Back**

If you depart from an abusive relationship, you may look back on all of the good times that you shared, especially if you love the person very much. You may recall that time they swept you off of your feet, or perhaps that time when they made you laugh so hard that you cried. During those moments, it can be very tempting to call or text them just to "say hi."

Don't do it! You're repeating the cycle of forgiving in hopes that it gets better. You've been there before, and it didn't end well for you. Trust yourself...know that you made the right decision when you left. There are some ways to reduce the temptations of contacting your former abuser:

- Delete their number from your phone- When scrolling through your phone, if you come across their name, you may be tempted to call. Or, change their name to "***Do Not Answer***."
- Get rid of the gifts they gave you- Those teddy bears, trinkets, cards, and other items they gave you will immediately remind you of them. Remember the saying 'out of sight, out of mind.'
- Toss the old photographs- Nothing brings back memories like a picture. This will likely be the toughest deletion of your life. There are two ways to do this. You can have a "cleansing" ceremony where you take the pictures and recite positive affirmations as you tear them and throw them away. Another way is to gather them all together, place them into an envelope, and drop them into the mailbox addressed to "The Universe."
- Stop inquiring about them to mutual friends- Unless they bring the person up, steer clear of mentioning them.

- <u>Stop driving by "your old place"</u> where the two of you used to hang out.
- <u>Delete them from your social networking circle</u>. This includes email addresses, friends' lists, and group contacts.
- <u>Meditate and focus on the peaceful and composed life you now lead without them</u>. (IMPORTANT: When meditating, do not allow your thoughts to drift into the drama that you endured during the relationship. That will only draw more dramatic situations to you. Only focus on the life you desire.)

(Above list excerpted from "The Secrets to Being an Unstoppable Woman")

**Be Alone**

Learn how to simply enjoy your own company. You've been through quite an ordeal and it's time to work on who you are. I decided not to date after my last abusive relationship and I was by myself for a couple of years. I enjoyed it very much! I mostly enjoyed the calmness of being alone with my thoughts without them being interrupted by "uh-oh, I'd better check in."

When you get to know yourself, spectacular things begin to happen. You value the opinions of others, but not more than your own. You enjoy silence when before it may have scared you. You can publicly be alone without fear of judgment. You can talk to yourself without feeling weird. You start to observe others from a more objective lens. You engage more fully in your interactions with others. You are intentional in your contributions to society. You sift through all the bull shit more easily and are okay with letting it go. You begin to create things that you never thought you could before. You no longer feel the need to be validated by another. You take better care of yourself. You no longer define yourself by your relationships. You become increasingly more self sufficient. And you realize that you are a freaking AWESOME human being!

Because this is your journey, the principles you have set in place should be the most important. You are enough, all by yourself sweet soul.

Staying Off the Beaten Path

# Building Healthy Relationships

8

Once, someone asked me to describe my ideal mate. My immediate impulse was to start listing bullet points that spelled out in detail what I wanted. But instead I paused for a moment, as I truly wanted to give the query some thought so that I could respond from the core of my authentic self. My response to them was, "I want someone who can make me smile in their absence." That felt real to me. It felt accurate. It felt...*just right.* Of course there are many details that encompass this vision, but in that moment, I didn't want to succumb to my knee jerk reaction.

In the process of coming up with a response, this made me realize two things. First, I became acutely aware that I was open to possibilities. Second, I recognized that it would take some time to invest in the right person and conscious effort to achieve my desired relationship.

## How Does it Look?

Once you're in a position where you feel ready to start a new union, it's imperative to first be clear about your idea of what a healthy relationship looks like. For many, it eludes them because they've spent their entire adult (and young adult) years trapped inside the bubble of abuse.

With fresh eyes, an open heart, and a renewed sense of self, let's get you on the path to being an active participant in the best relationship of your life.

On the pages that follow, you will notice two tables. Each has multiple attributes that encompass various elements of a healthy relationship. The first table specifically asks about what it is that you want from your healthy relationship. The second table asks about specific traits that you have to offer your healthy relationship.

Circle the top 5 attributes in each table that best represent your idea of what your healthy relationship will look like. There are blank spaces below each table for you to fill in elements that may not be present, but are important to you.

## What Do You Want **From** Your Relationship?

| Open Communication | Humor | Career Support |
|---|---|---|
| Emotional Support | Trust | Protection |
| Faith Commonality | Romance | Sexual Compatibility |
| Monogamy | Loving Ear | Encouragement |
| Quality Time | Financial Security | Honesty |
| Active Parenting | Health Conscious | Social Conscious |
| | | |

## What Do You Have to **Offer** Your Relationship?

| Open Communication | Humor | Career Support |
|---|---|---|
| Emotional Support | Trust | Protection |
| Faith Commonality | Romance | Sexual Compatibility |
| Monogamy | Loving Ear | Encouragement |
| Quality Time | Financial Security | Honesty |
| Active Parenting | Health Conscious | Social Conscious |
| | | |

Now that you have finished this assessment, complete the following sentences using what you've selected above:

*My name is _____, and my healthy relationship offers me _____, _____,*

_____, _____,
*and* _____.

*My name is* _____, *and I offer my healthy relationship*
_____, _____,
_____, _____,
*and* _____.

There's something that I want you to notice about the previous tables. Each attribute was grounded in positivity. Those are the things that we want to focus on when creating our ideal union.

## The Dating Process

Now that we're clear about what our individual healthy relationship looks like, it's time to actively be part of the process. Something that I've noticed in recent years is the varying degrees of ideas of what dating actually is. Some ideas of dating include:

- Having sex with someone and going out occasionally with them
- Going out with just one person at a time without sex
- Going out with multiple people, without sex

It's important to be clear about what dating looks like to you. My idea of dating is pretty simple – when you choose to go out with a person, you're not committed until you have the "Commitment Conversation." There seems to be a common thread of people assuming that they are part of a committed union after so many dates. Leaving something as important as commitment up to assumption can be misleading and even dangerous.

Here's how to alleviate that trap. During the first 2 dates, there are some preliminary questions that should be asked not only to get an idea of how your date views the dating process, but how they operate as a human being in this world.

1. What are some causes that are important to you?
2. What's your religious affiliation, if any?
3. Do you like children? Do you have any? Do you want any?
4. What constitutes a committed relationship to you?
5. What do you like to do for fun?
6. Have you ever been in a committed relationship? If so, what did you like or dislike about it?
7. Have you ever had your heart broken?
8. Have you ever broken anybody's heart?
9. What are you currently looking for in a relationship?
10. What's your relationship like with your family?
11. What are your career goals?
12. What area of your life would you like to improve the most?

*Please do NOT ask all of these questions as if the person is being interrogated under a hot light!* I wouldn't even suggest asking all of these questions on the first date. Allow time to process what it is that you've learned thus far before you proceed through the list. Also, be sure to ask the questions that are the most important to you in the very beginning. Start with your deal breakers, if any. You may not even get to the second date.

In addition, I suggest making it very clear that when you're ready to commit to the relationship, you will say so. Perhaps you can make the statement, "When I'm ready to commit to someone, I will verbally make it known. Until then, there's no commitment on my part." Pause. Do not say anything else until you have received a response to that statement. Saying anything else behind that may steer the conversation away from this crucial point in the dating process. If you get a blank stare, or if they're otherwise non responsive, then you may ask, "What do you think about that?"

The goal is to be in alignment when it comes to being clear about the intersection of the end of dating, and the beginning of commitment.

**We're Committed, Now What?**

When you have mutually decided to commit to each other, be sure that your version of a healthy relationship remains lucid throughout the union. You can do this by periodically checking in to see if your relationship is still meeting your standards. This isn't something that needs to be presented to your partner; it's just a check-in process you should do for yourself. Some of the elements of a healthy relationship include:

- Learning and growing through your conflicts
- They speak to you with respect
- You feel emotionally safe with them
- You can name multiple aspects of their personality that please you
- Economic statuses are shared
- They respect your boundaries and you feel safe expressing what they are
- Your privacy is respected
- You feel safe living as an individual in addition to being part of a union
- Your partner shows genuine concern for things that bring

you worry
- You feel safe being your most authentic self, even when it doesn't necessarily gel with them
- You're able to maintain your belief system and sense of self comfortably
- You don't feel as if your psyche is being played with
- You feel beautiful in their eyes
- The idea of being vulnerable with them doesn't scare you
- You're able to disagree without it escalating to any form of abuse
- The things that you enjoy doing aren't made fun of
- They encourage you to pursue your dreams and passions
- They share some of your recreational interests
- They're comfortable being around your friends and family
- They are proud of your accomplishments
- You don't feel the need to check in out of fear that there will be unsafe consequences
- You don't feel pressured to participate in things that you're uncomfortable with
- You're not excessively being accused of being unfaithful

As the relationship changes and evolves, you may modify your behavior, but don't ever modify your _values_.

**It Starts With You**
You are responsible for setting the boundaries as you see fit. You've been through a lot and repeating an abusive cycle does not serve you well. Now that you're part of a healthy relationship, let's work on keeping you healthy as well. To keep your mind sharp, body fit, and spirits high, practice some of

these activities on a regular basis:

- o Exercise
- o Eat healthy foods
- o Single tasking (No excessive multi-tasking)
- o Take vacations
- o Do mindful meditation
- o Be gentle with yourself when you make mistakes
- o Say "no" to less pressing tasks and favors
- o Connect with who you are authentically
- o Trust your decision-making process
- o Be intentional for at least 1 hour per day in an area that you want to improve
- o Ask for help when needed

Remember that healing is on the other side of vulnerability. The only way to guarantee that your future self will be better is to invest in your present self right now. In order to fully live your life without regrets, know yourself and love yourself.

If You Leave, I Will Kill You!

# Resources

9

1. **American Bar Association Commission on Domestic and Sexual Violence**: The Commission seeks to address domestic and sexual violence from a legal perspective. Its mission is to increase access to justice for survivors of DV, sexual assault, and stalking by engaging the interest and support of members of the legal profession.

2. **Asian & Pacific Islander Institute on Domestic Violence**: The API Institute is a national resource center focused on gender-based violence (DV, sexual violence, and trafficking) in Asian and Pacific Islander communities. It addresses these issues by increasing awareness, strengthening community strategies for prevention and intervention, and promoting research and policy.

3. **Battered Women's Justice Project**: BWJP offers DV-related training, technical assistance, and consultation to members of the criminal and civil justice systems. The Project analyzes and advocates for effective policing, prosecuting, sentencing, and monitoring of perpetrators of domestic violence.

4. **Child Welfare League of America**: CWLA is comprised of a coalition of hundreds of private and public agencies serving at-risk children and families. The League works to advances policies and strategies that promote safe, stable families and assist children, youth, and adults whose families don't meet those criteria.

5. **Equality Now**: Working with grassroots organizations and activists, Equality Now seeks to protect and promote the human rights of women and girls all over the world

by documenting violence and discrimination against women and mobilizing efforts to stop these abuses.

6. **Futures Without Violence**: FWV aims to advance the health, stability, education, and security of women, men, girls, and boys worldwide. To that end, the organization was a big player in developing the **Violence Against Women Act** (passed by Congress in 1994) and continues to work with policy makers and train professionals (doctors, nurses, athletic coaches, and judges) to improve responses to DV and educate people about the importance of healthy relationships.

7. **INCITE! Women of Color Against Violence**: INCITE! describes itself as a "national activist organization of radical feminists of color advancing a movement to end violence against women of color and our communities." Comprised of grassroots chapters across the U.S., the organization works with groups of women of color and their communities to develop political projects that address the violence women of color may experience both within their communities and individual lives.

8. **Institute of Domestic Violence in the African American Community**: Run out of the University of Minnesota, the Institute has several clearly defined objectives: to further scholarship in the area of African American violence; to provide outreach and technical assistance to African American communities experiencing violence; to raise awareness about the impacts of violence in African American communities; to influence public policy; and to organize violence-related trainings on local and national scales.

9. **Jewish Women International**: JWI seeks to empower women and girls through economic literacy, community trainings, and education about healthy relationships. The organization aims to end violence against women by advocating for policies focused on violence prevention and reproductive rights, developing philanthropic initiatives along similar lines, and inspiring "the next generation of leaders" by recognizing and celebrating women's achievements.

10. **Manavi**: Manavi, which means "primal woman" in Sanskrit, is a women's rights organization committed to ending violence and exploitation committed against South Asian women living in the U.S. The organization provides direct service to survivors of violence, grassroots organization aimed at changing communities, and awareness programs on local and national levels.

11. **Mending the Sacred Hoop**: Relying on grassroots efforts, MSH works to end violence against Native women and children. Their overarching mission is "restore the sovereignty and leadership of Native women"; they seek to do so through technical assistance projects and organizing Native women to advocate for the end of violence.

12. **National Center on Domestic and Sexual Violence**: A national training organization, NCDSV works to influence national policy and provides customized training and consultation to professionals working in fields that might influence domestic violence.

13. **National Coalition Against Domestic Violence**: NCADV works from the premise that violence against women and children results from the abuse of power on all scales,

from intimate relationships to societal issues like sexism, racism, and homophobia. Therefore, NCADV advocates for major societal changes that will eliminate both personal and social violence for all people by building coalitions, supporting shelter programs, providing public education, and developing policies and legislation.

14. **National Domestic Violence Hotline**: The Hotline provides 24-hour support and crisis intervention to victims and survivors of DV through safety planning, advocacy, resources, and a supportive ear.

15. **National Latino Alliance for the Elimination of Domestic Violence (ALIANZA)**: Allianza is a network of organizations addressing the needs of Latino/a families and communities by promoting understanding, dialogue, and solutions that aim to eliminate domestic violence in Latino communities.

16. **National Network to End Domestic Violence**: NNEDV is an advocacy organization made up of state domestic violence coalitions and allied organizations and individuals. The organization works closely with its members to understand the needs of domestic violence victims and programs, and then voices those needs to national policymakers.

17. **No More**: No More arose from the desire to unite the diverse array of groups working to end domestic violence and sexual assault. **Hundreds of representatives** from the violence and assault prevention field collaborated to develop a symbol that unites all people working to end these issues, with the end goal of ratcheting up public awareness. The blue vanishing point symbolizes "zero,"

representing the organization's desire to reach zero incidences of domestic violence and sexual assault.

18. **The Northwest Network**: Founded by lesbian survivors of domestic, the NW Network works to end abuse in lesbian, gay, bisexual, and transgender communities and to support and empower all survivors through education and advocacy.

19. **Rape, Abuse, and Incest National Network (RAINN)**: RAINN is the nation's largest anti-sexual violence organization. The Network created and operates the National Sexual Assault Hotline (800.656.HOPE) and operates the Department of Defense's **Safe Helpline**. The organization also runs programs to prevent sexual violence, assist survivors, and ensure that rapists are brought to justice.

20. **V-Day**: Founded by author Eve Ensler and activists from New York City, V-Day is a global activist movement seeking to end violence against women and girls. The organization stages creative events— most famously, THE VAGINA MONOLOGUES and the documentary UNTIL THE VIOLENCE STOPS — to increase awareness, raise funds, and support other anti-violence organizations.

Notes:

_____

_____

_____

_____

_____

_____

_____

_____

_____

_____

_____

_____

_____

_____

_____

If You Leave, I Will Kill You!

Erika Gilchrist is an Award-Winning Speaker, 9X published author, and community advocate specializing in women's issues and IPV (Intimate Partner Violence). Assaulted as a little girl, sleeping in a van as a young adult, and living in a women's shelter, Ms. Gilchrist has earn the title of *"The Unstoppable Woman."* She is regarded as one of the most energizing, engaging, and captivating speakers in the industry. As a published author of 9 books, she gives a powerful voice to those who struggle to be heard and offers real solutions to end the epidemic. She's been featured as one of the *"15 Most Powerful Women on the South Side of Chicago,"* CLTV, and Rolling Out Magazine.

To the 5 year old me, I want to say:

*"You are beautiful just the way you are. There may be times when you don't believe it – like when your face has severe acne, or when you gain 40 pounds, or when the person you love hits you.*

*You are beautiful, and courageous, and unstoppable. Remember to always seek the voice in your head that tells you to do the right thing, even when it scares you. That is your higher self.*

*Daddy may not physically be here, but his loving spirit and strong nature lives inside you. Use that strength when you're feeling weak. Be kind to others because they need you too. Erika...You. Are. Beautiful!"*

If You Leave, I Will Kill You!

# Resources

If You Leave, I Will Kill You!

www.ingramcontent.com/pod-product-compliance
Lightning Source LLC
Chambersburg PA
CBHW021342090426
42742CB00008B/715